WHERE WE LIVE

By Susan Hoe

Science and curriculum consultant:
Debra Voege, M.A., science curriculum resource teacher

Gareth Stevens
Publishing

Please visit our web site at www.garethstevens.com
For a free catalog describing our list of high-quality books, call 1-800-542-2595 (USA) or 1-800-387-3178 (Canada).
Our fax: 1-877-542-2596

Library of Congress Cataloging-in-Publication Data available upon request from publisher.

ISBN-10: 0-8368-9207-0   ISBN-13: 978-0-8368-9207-9 (lib. bdg.)
ISBN-10: 0-8368-9334-4   ISBN-13: 978-0-8368-9334-2 (softcover)

This edition first published in 2009 by
Gareth Stevens Publishing
A Weekly Reader® Company
1 Reader's Digest Road
Pleasantville, NY 10570-7000 USA

This U.S. edition copyright © 2009 by Gareth Stevens, Inc. Original edition copyright © 2008 by ticktock Media Ltd. First published in
Great Britain in 2008 by ticktock Media Ltd., Unit 2, Orchard Business Centre, North Farm Road, Tunbridge Wells, Kent, TN2 3XF

Gareth Stevens Senior Managing Editor: Lisa M. Herrington
Gareth Stevens Creative Director: Lisa Donovan
Gareth Stevens Art Director: Ken Crossland
Gareth Stevens Associate Editor: Amanda Hudson

Picture credits (t=top; b=bottom; c=center; l=left; r=right):
Bananastock: 17tr; Corbis: 21b; Cultura Limited/SuperStock: 6t; Digital Vision Ltd/SuperStock: 12br; David R. Frazier Photolibrary, Inc./
Alamy: 15bl; Chris George/Alamy: 19b; Getmapping PLC: 24c; Image100/SuperStock: 7b; Images of Birmingham/Alamy: 10b; iStock:
10t, 17bl, 17br, 22t, 25b; Ulli Seer/Getty Images: 5t; Shutterstock: 1, 4t, 4b, 6b, 8, 17tl, 20, 24b, 24b, 25t, 25c, 27 all; Justin Spain: 22b,
23; Hayley Terry: 5b, 6b (map), 11t, 11b, 12b, 13, 15br, 31t; Tim Thirlaway: 28, 29; ticktock Media Archive: 30b; Brett Walker;
www.mapart.co.uk: 7t, 14, 15t, 16, 18, 19t, 26, 31b.

Every effort has been made to trace the copyright holders for the photos used in this book, and the publisher apologizes in advance
for any unintentional omissions. We would be pleased to insert the appropriate acknowledgments in any subsequent edition of this
publication.

Printed in the United States of America

1 2 3 4 5 6 7 8 9 10 09 08

Contents

What Is a Map? 4

Why Do We Need Maps? 6

Mapping Your Bedroom 8

Mapping Your Town 10

Using Your Town Map 12

Mapping Your Country 14

Mapping the World 16

Mapping a Country in Africa: Sudan 18

Mapping Grace's Village 20

Measuring for Maps 22

Mapping With Computers 24

Mapping African Animals 26

Making a Playground Map 28

Glossary 30

Index 32

Words in **bold** are defined in the glossary.

What Is a Map?

A **map** is a special drawing. This kind of drawing shows parts of an area. The area is drawn as seen from above.

This area can be as big as the state where you live. Or it can be as small as your bedroom!

Making a Map of an Island

Map Key

 Trees/Woods

 Roads/footpaths

 Gray-roofed building

 Red-roofed building

 Pier

 Gardens

Maps help us see things as if we were directly above them.

In this book, we are going to see how maps show us places where people live. But first, let's look at some of the ways that maps can help us.

Find the gray-roofed buildings on the map.

Now look for them in the photo.

Why Do We Need Maps?

Maps help us find our way around. They give us all kinds of information about where we live.

A map can help you get from one place to another. It can show you where you are. It can show where to go and how to get there.

Weather Map of the United States

This map shows what the weather will be like where you live.

Can you tell what kinds of weather this map is showing?

Map of the World

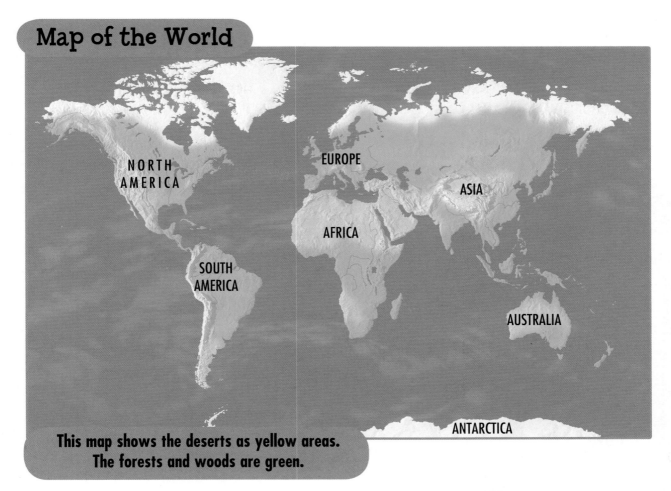

NORTH AMERICA

EUROPE

ASIA

AFRICA

SOUTH AMERICA

AUSTRALIA

ANTARCTICA

This map shows the deserts as yellow areas. The forests and woods are green.

Maps teach us important facts about places. We can learn about places close to home or on the other side of the world.

Maps can show whether land is flat or has hills. They can show where people and animals live. We can also learn what **crops** are grown. We can see what sorts of things are made in a place.

Maps are handy and easy to use. They can show us huge areas in a small amount of space. We can take them just about anywhere!

Mapping Your Bedroom

Maps show a place as if you were looking down on it. That place can be a country or a town. It can even be your bedroom!

A 3–D room

This room is a **three-dimensional (3-D)** space. The room and the things in it are solid. They have length, width, and **depth**.

A 2-D Map

A map is a flat, **two-dimensional (2-D)** drawing of a space. In a map, all the objects look flat. They have only length and width.

To create a map, we draw all the flat shapes on a piece of paper.

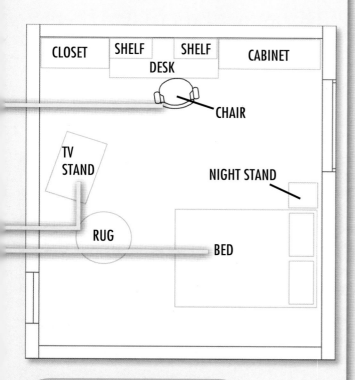

A 2–D map of a 3–D room

This map shows you the room and everything in it.

Find the rug.   Find the chair.

Making the Map

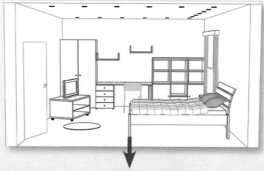

This drawing of the room was made from photos.

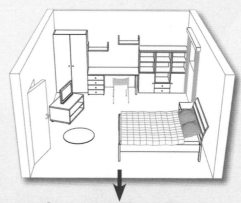

Pretend you are able to float up above the room. Imagine looking down on it.

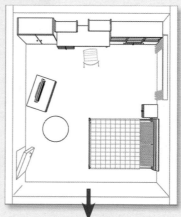

If you are right above the room, it looks flat. This is the view we use to make a 2-D map.

Mapping Your Town

You saw how to make a map of a room. You can also use maps to show larger areas. When you look at a map of your town, you can see interesting places. You can also figure out how to find them.

A Photo of a 3-D Town

Hospital

Museum

Library

School

Outdoor pool

This photo shows interesting places in a town. Without a map, it might be hard to find them!

A 2-D Map of the Town

This map shows where the important places are found. It uses different **symbols** to stand for each place. The map has a key. This **map key** is also called a legend. It tells you what each symbol means.

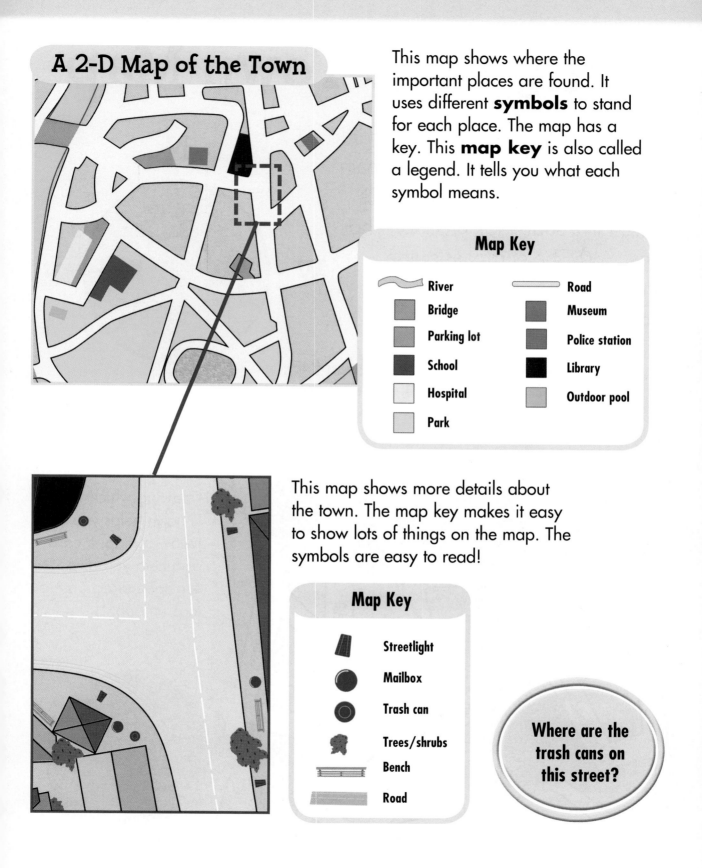

Map Key

～	River	▭	Road
▪	Bridge	▪	Museum
▪	Parking lot	▪	Police station
▪	School	▪	Library
▪	Hospital	▪	Outdoor pool
▪	Park		

This map shows more details about the town. The map key makes it easy to show lots of things on the map. The symbols are easy to read!

Map Key

- Streetlight
- Mailbox
- Trash can
- Trees/shrubs
- Bench
- Road

Where are the trash cans on this street?

Using Your Town Map

A map usually has a compass guide. The guide points to the four main directions on the map. It points north (N), south (S), east (E), and west (W). The compass guide shown here is called a **compass rose**.

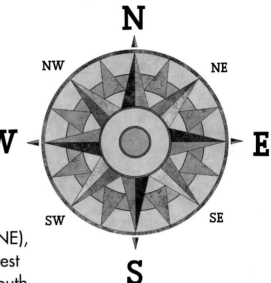

A compass rose may also show northeast (NE), southeast (SE), southwest (SW), and northwest (NW). These are found in between north, south, east, and west.

Knowing which way is north helps you follow a map. It can also help you give someone directions to a school!

YOU ARE HERE

Bridge Street

Barker Street

Victoria Avenue

Claremont Road

St. John's Hill

Swan Hill

Priory Road

Quarry Road

School

Buildings in a Town

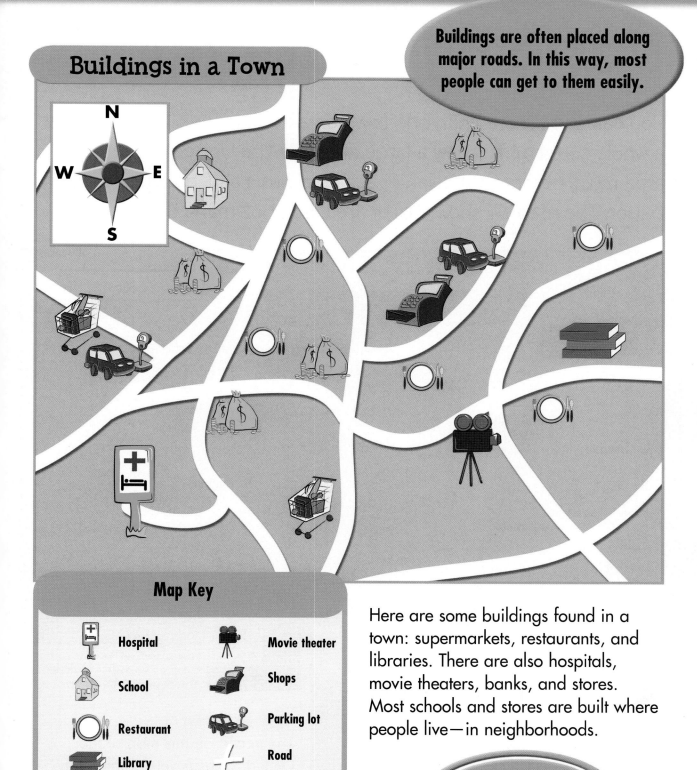

Buildings are often placed along major roads. In this way, most people can get to them easily.

Map Key

Hospital		Movie theater	
School		Shops	
Restaurant		Parking lot	
Library		Road	
Bank		Supermarket	

Here are some buildings found in a town: supermarkets, restaurants, and libraries. There are also hospitals, movie theaters, banks, and stores. Most schools and stores are built where people live—in neighborhoods.

Find the supermarkets and the school.

Mapping Your Country

You can show more than one town on a map. In fact, you can show a whole country! To show a large area, like the United States, the area must be drawn smaller, or scaled down, to fit on a piece of paper. The map will show lots of area, but not many details.

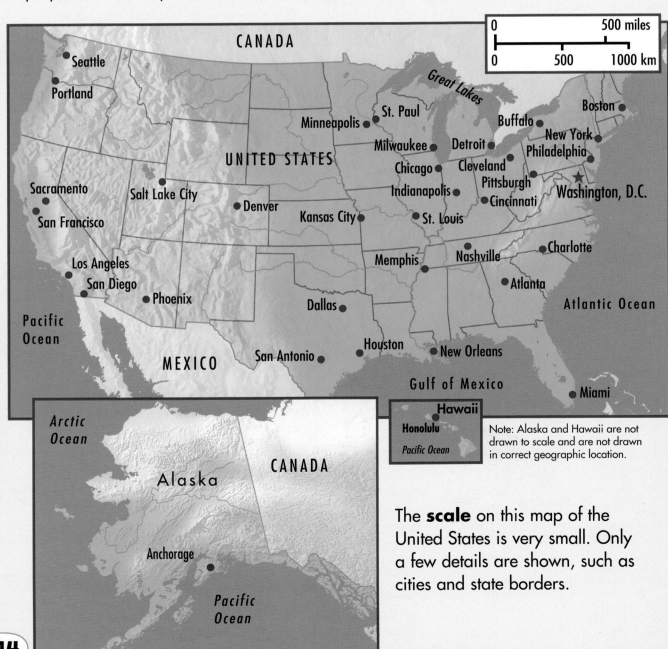

Note: Alaska and Hawaii are not drawn to scale and are not drawn in correct geographic location.

The **scale** on this map of the United States is very small. Only a few details are shown, such as cities and state borders.

This map shows New York state. It has a larger scale than the United States map does. You can see land features, such as rivers. You can see more cities.

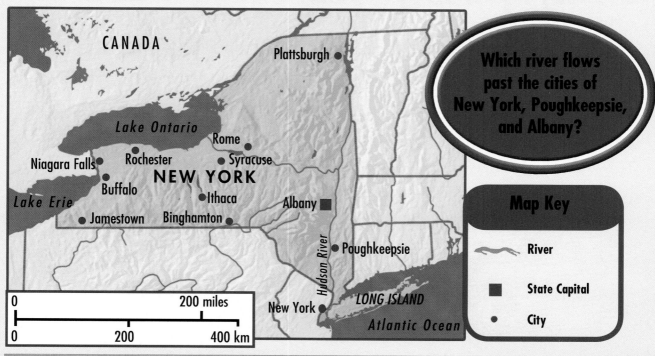

CANADA

Plattsburgh

Lake Ontario

Rome

Niagara Falls   Rochester   Syracuse

NEW YORK

Buffalo   Ithaca   Albany

Lake Erie

Jamestown   Binghamton

Hudson River   Poughkeepsie

LONG ISLAND

New York

Atlantic Ocean

| 0 | | 200 miles |
| 0 | 200 | 400 km |

Which river flows past the cities of New York, Poughkeepsie, and Albany?

Map Key

~~~~ River

■ State Capital

• City

Towns and Water Routes

Many towns were built next to rivers, lakes, and oceans.

Water routes help ships move goods from place to place. They help people travel more easily. Many towns that were built near water have grown into major cities. New Orleans (shown above) is a good example.

This map shows the mighty Mississippi River. It also shows towns that grew along its banks.

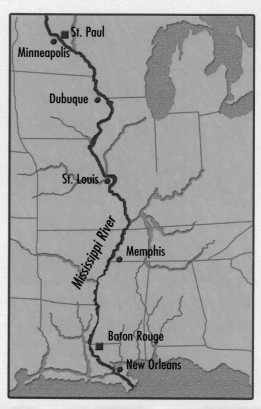

St. Paul

Minneapolis

Dubuque

St. Louis

Mississippi River

Memphis

Baton Rouge

New Orleans

Mapping the World

The United States is part of North America. That is a large area of land called a **continent**. There are seven continents. The continents are North America, South America, Africa, Europe, Asia, Australia, and Antarctica. Maps come in different forms. Two of those forms are **physical maps** and **political maps**.

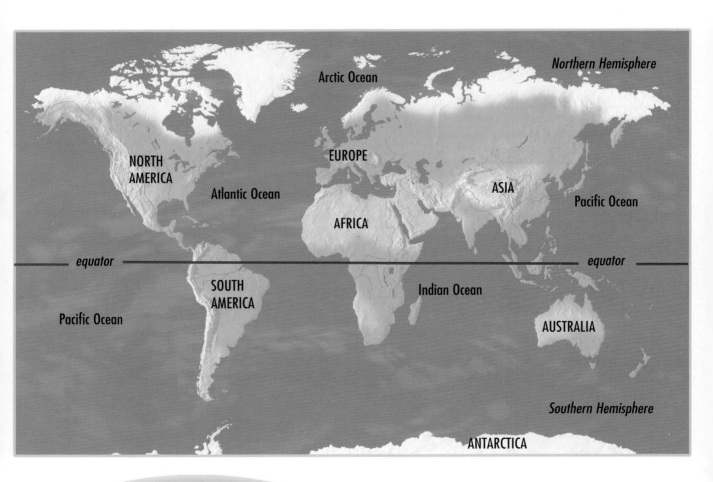

Northern Hemisphere

Arctic Ocean

NORTH AMERICA

Atlantic Ocean

EUROPE

ASIA

Pacific Ocean

AFRICA

equator

equator

SOUTH AMERICA

Indian Ocean

Pacific Ocean

AUSTRALIA

Southern Hemisphere

ANTARCTICA

This physical map shows natural features of the continents. These features include bodies of water, mountains, forests, and deserts.

The **equator** is an imaginary line. It divides Earth into two halves. One half is the Northern Hemisphere. The other half is the Southern Hemisphere. North America is north of the equator.

One Continent, Many Countries

A political map shows how continents are divided into countries. People who live in the same continent often speak different languages.

A political map of North America

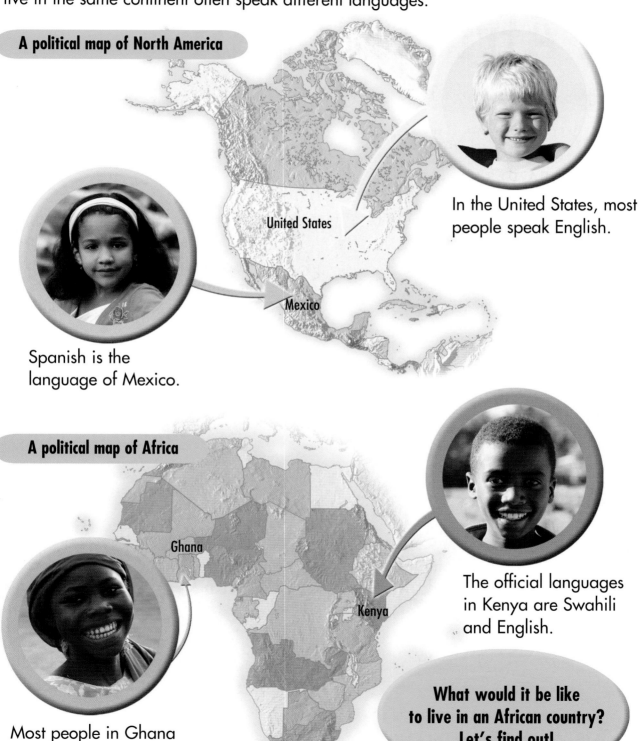

In the United States, most people speak English.

Spanish is the language of Mexico.

A political map of Africa

The official languages in Kenya are Swahili and English.

Most people in Ghana speak English.

What would it be like to live in an African country? Let's find out!

17

Mapping a Country in Africa: Sudan

A physical map of Africa

Africa is a large continent. It has more than fifty countries. It also has many natural features.

SAHARA DESERT

Nile River

Niger River

SUDAN

Congo River

Zambezi River

The map key shows that Africa has dry deserts and rain forest jungles. It has grasslands and mountains. Africa also has four main rivers. They are the Nile, Congo, Niger, and Zambezi.

Map Key

- Grasslands
- Desert
- Rain forest
- Mountains
- Lake

Sudan is the largest country in Africa. Its land features range from dry deserts to mountains and grasslands. The Blue Nile and the White Nile rivers meet at Khartoum. Here, they form the mighty Nile River.

Find Khartoum, the capital city of Sudan, on the map.

A physical map of Sudan

LIBYA

EGYPT

Red Sea

Nubian Desert

Port Sudan

Nile River

CHAD

Omdurman

★ **Khartoum**

SUDAN

White Nile

Blue Nile

ETHIOPIA

CENTRAL AFRICAN REPUBLIC

Mt. Kinyet ▲

A World Apart

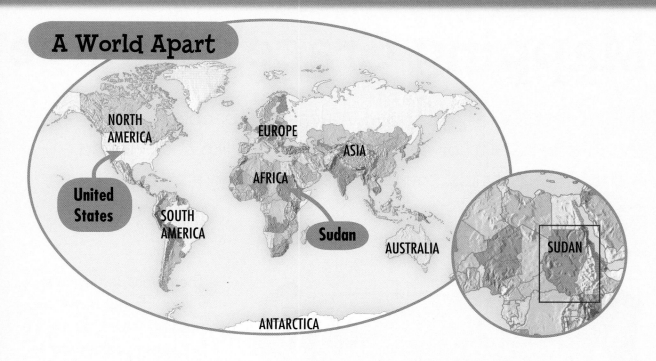

Sudan and the United States are on different continents. They are thousands of miles apart. Yet they have some of the same kinds of land. Both have deserts, mountains, and flat, grassy plains.

Desert makes up much more land in Sudan than in the United States. This is why the most important cities in Sudan, like Khartoum (below), grew up along rivers.

The Blue Nile flows through Khartoum.

Mapping Grace's Village

This is Grace's village in Sudan, Africa. Fifty people live in the village. Instead of wood or brick houses like those found in the United States, the villagers live in big huts. The huts are called **tukuls**.

The homes in Grace's village do not have running water. So Grace has an important job to do. She must collect water from the well for her family every morning.

The village map uses symbols that stand for parts of Grace's community. The map key helps you understand what the symbols mean.

Grace's Village

The people in Grace's village grow fruits and vegetables in gardens. They grow pumpkins, tomatoes, corn, and a type of grain called sorghum. They raise goats in pens for milk and meat.

Map Key

Tukul		Goat pen	
School huts		Vegetable garden	
Well		Tree	

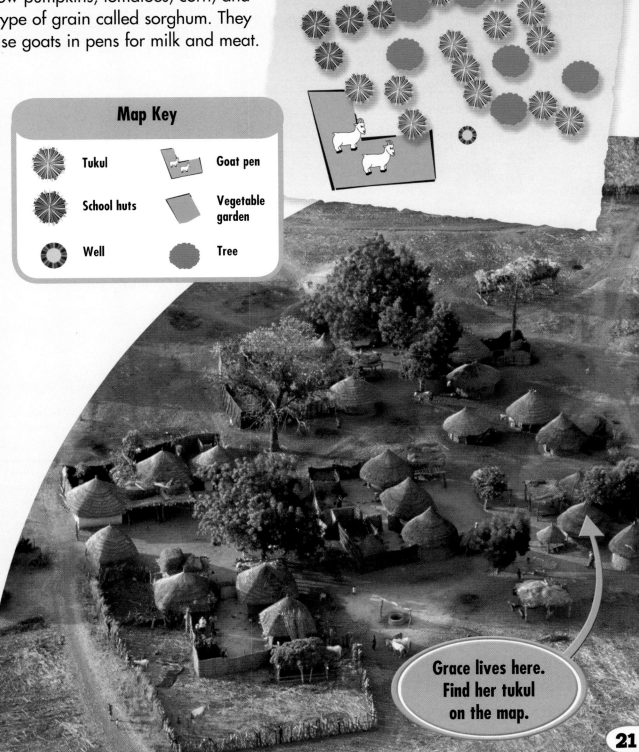

Grace lives here. Find her tukul on the map.

Measuring for Maps

Before you can draw a map, you must figure out the size and shape of the area. This means figuring out how to measure large areas.

This man uses special equipment to measure distances between points.

Mapmakers use their measurements to draw their maps. The maps on these pages show an amusement park.

Scale: Shrinking to Fit

Mapmakers gather all their measurements. Then they figure out how to fit them onto a piece of paper. So they shrink, or scale down, the real measurements to make a map.

0	50 feet
15 meters	

This map shows a fairly large area. It uses a scale of 50 feet (15 meters). Many objects can be seen, but they are quite small.

Different scales can be used to map the same area. A different scale can change what you see. Some maps show large areas on a sheet of paper. Other maps show smaller areas, so the same objects look bigger and have more features.

The map scale is like a ruler. It shows the connection between distance on the map and distance on the ground. This way you can figure out real distances on the map.

0   25 feet
━━━━━━━
         8 meters

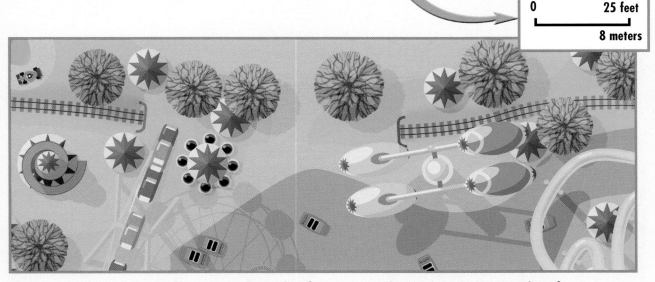

This map shows a smaller area than the first map. This map uses a scale of 25 feet (8 m). You see fewer objects on this map, but they seem closer.

0   15 feet
━━━━━━━
         5 meters

This map has the largest scale. It shows an even smaller area. You see fewer objects, but they seem even closer.

Mapping With Computers

Many years ago, people had to travel to figure out the shape of the land. Today, mapmakers use computer equipment.

Mapmakers can take many photographs of the ground from an airplane.

This photograph shows the ground as seen from the airplane.

Pictures and measurements are taken from an airplane and sent to computers. The computers use the pictures to draw maps.

Satellites also take pictures of Earth from space.

A satellite circling Earth

Pictures are taken from space, too. The pictures are sent back to Earth. They are put together to make full pictures of our planet, like the one shown here. These pictures can then be turned into maps.

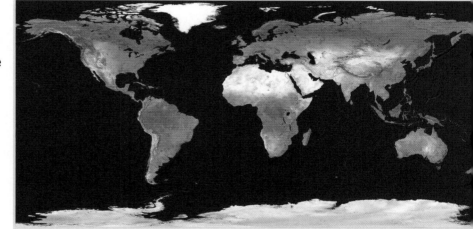

Changing Maps

Satellites can produce road maps that help you find your way. These maps change as you move. The maps are called **GPS (Global Positioning System)** maps.

A GPS map at work in a car

Mapping African Animals

Africa is home to thousands of kinds of animals. Some of the animals live in jungles. Others live on grassy plains or in rivers. Here's how you can create a map that shows where they live!

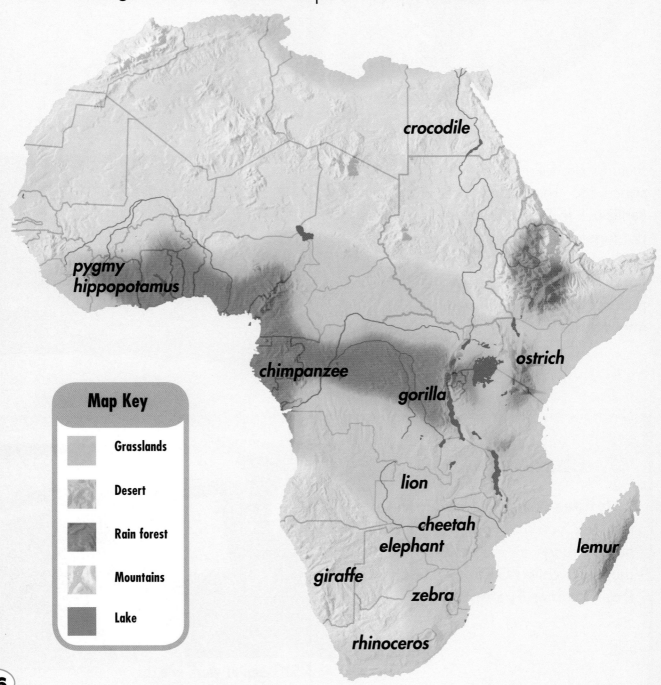

crocodile

pygmy hippopotamus

chimpanzee

gorilla

ostrich

lion

cheetah

elephant

giraffe

zebra

lemur

rhinoceros

Map Key

Grasslands

Desert

Rain forest

Mountains

Lake

How to Make a Map of the Animals of Africa

1. Copy the map of Africa on page 26 onto a blank sheet of paper. You can also use thin paper to trace the map.

2. Now make an animal map key. Include pictures of the animals shown below.

3. The map on page 26 shows some places where these animals live. Use that map as a guide. Draw your own animal pictures on your map of Africa. Be sure to draw the animals so they look like the ones in your animal map key. You have now made a map of where African animals live!

Animal Map Key

lemur	gorilla	pygmy hippopotamus	cheetah
giraffe	zebra	rhinoceros	elephant
ostrich	lion	crocodile	chimpanzee

Making a Playground Map

Playgrounds are fun places to visit. Make a map of your dream playground. Include all of your favorite playground activities! Make a map key so your friends can find all the great things in your playground.

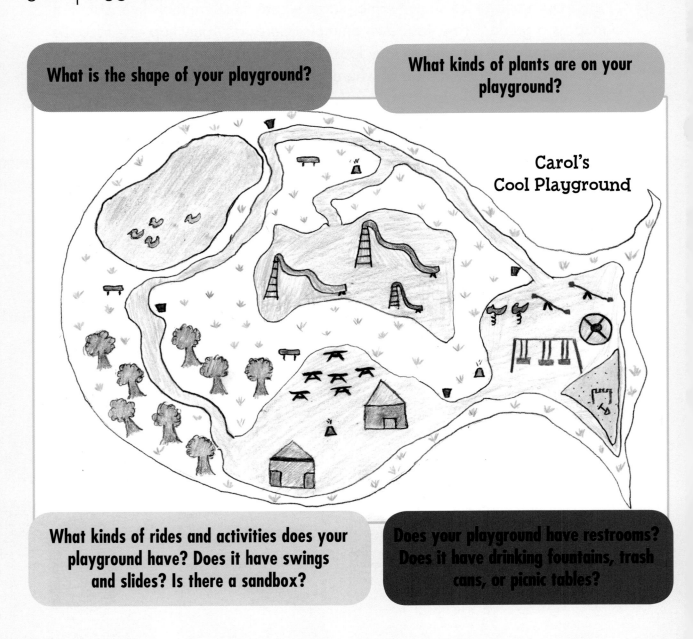

What is the shape of your playground?

What kinds of plants are on your playground?

Carol's Cool Playground

What kinds of rides and activities does your playground have? Does it have swings and slides? Is there a sandbox?

Does your playground have restrooms? Does it have drinking fountains, trash cans, or picnic tables?

Step 1

Draw the shape of your playground on a piece of paper.

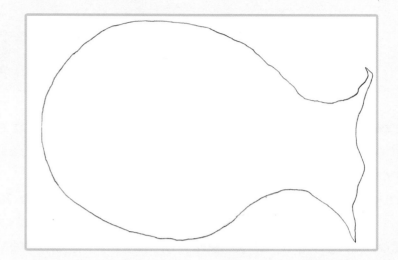

Step 2

Make up symbols for all the items you want to include on your map. Be sure you leave enough space between the symbols. Draw in paths and grassy areas, too.

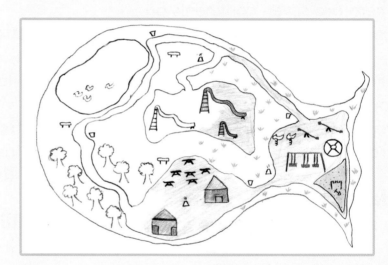

Step 3

Color your playground map and give it a name.

Step 4

Make your map key using the symbols on your map.

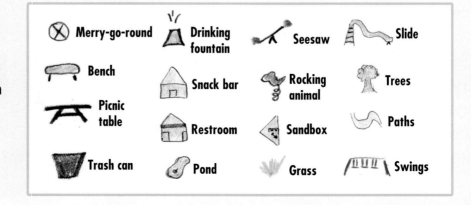

Merry-go-round   Drinking fountain   Seesaw   Slide

Bench   Snack bar   Rocking animal   Trees

Picnic table   Restroom   Sandbox   Paths

Trash can   Pond   Grass   Swings

Glossary

compass rose: a drawing that shows directions on a map: north (N), south (S), east (E) and west (W)

continent: a large body of land. There are seven continents on Earth.

crops: plants that are grown for food or other purposes. Fruits, vegetables, grains, and nuts are crops.

depth: the length from the top of a space or an object to the bottom

equator: an imaginary line that circles Earth halfway between the North and South poles. The top half is the Northern Hemisphere. The bottom half is the Southern Hemisphere.

GPS (Global Positioning System): an instrument that shows how to get to a place. In a moving car, the instrument shows the driver directions on a screen.

map: a picture or chart showing features of an area

map key: the space on a map that shows the meaning of any pictures or colors on the map

physical maps: maps that show rivers, oceans, mountains, and other land features.

political maps: maps that show countries or states. Borders outline each area.

satellites: objects sent into space that circle and study Earth or other bodies in space. They then send information back to Earth.

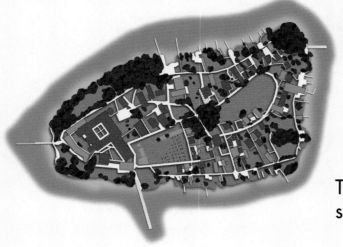

two-dimensional (2-D): appearing as a flat shape with only length and width

water route: a way to get people and goods from one place to another by boat or ship. The water route can be a river, stream or open ocean.

scale: the amount by which the measurement of an area is shrunk to fit on a map. The map scale is a drawing or symbol that tells how to measure distances on a map.

symbols: pictures or drawings that stand for different things

three-dimensional (3-D): appearing as a solid thing that has length, width, and depth

tukuls: huts found in parts of Africa. The walls are made of mud. The cone-shaped roofs are made of straw.

Index

A
Africa 16, 18–21
  animal map 26–27
  physical map 16, 18
  political map 17
airplanes 24
amusement parks 22–23
animals 26–27

B
bedrooms 4, 8–9
Blue Nile River 18, 19
buildings 13

C
compass guide 12, 13
compass rose 12, 13
Congo River 18
continents 16–17
countries 14–15, 17
crops 7, 21

D
drawing maps 22–23

E
equator 16

G
Ghana 17
Global Positioning System
  (GPS) 25
Grace's village 20–21

K
Kenya 17
Khartoum 18, 19

L
languages 17
legend (map key) 5, 11,
  13, 18, 21, 26, 29
length 8, 9

M
map key (legend) 5, 11,
  13, 18, 21, 26, 29
mapmaking 9, 22–25,
  26–27, 28–29
measuring areas 22
Mexico 17
Mississippi River 15

N
New York State 15
Niger River 18
Nile River 18
North America 16, 17
Northern Hemisphere 16

P
physical maps 16, 18
playgrounds 28–29
political maps 16, 17

R
rivers 15, 18
road maps 6, 25

S
satellites 25
scale 14–15, 22–23
Southern Hemisphere 16
Sudan 18–21
surveying 22
symbols 11, 20, 29

T
three-dimensional spaces
  8–9, 10
towns 10–12
tukuls 20, 21
two-dimensional drawings
  9, 11

U
United States 14–15, 17,
  19

W
water collection 20
water routes 15
weather maps 6
White Nile River 18
world map 7, 16, 19

Z
Zambezi River 18